THE
SIMPLE
PARENTING
GUIDE
TO
TECHNOLOGY

PRACTICAL ADVICE ON SMARTPHONES, GAMING, AND SOCIAL MEDIA IN JUST 40 PAGES

Joshua Wayne

This book is not a substitute for medical advice, diagnosis or treatment. If you need immediate assistance, or if you and your family are in crisis, please contact a qualified mental health provider in your area, contact your statewide crisis hotline, or take your child to your local emergency room.

ISBN 978-1-7344292-0-6 (paperback)
ISBN 978-1-7344292-1-3 (ebook)

Published by BK Publishing
SPGbooks.com

GET YOUR FREE RESOURCES FOR PARENTING KIDS IN THE DIGITAL AGE AT SPGBOOKS.COM/TECH

To get all of the tech links and resources mentioned in this book PLUS free, simple parenting tools to help your kids make good decisions and thrive in school and life visit: **SPGbooks.com/tech**

CONTENTS

INTRODUCTION

THIS BOOK REVOLVES AROUND A SINGLE CORE PREMISE: **KIDS AND TEENS NEED LIMITS ON THEIR USE OF TECHNOLOGY**.

Research conducted by *Common Sense Media* found the average teen spends nearly *seven and a half hours a day* in front of a screen doing non-schoolwork-related activities. Over the course of a year, that's a staggering four months spent on devices. It's hard to argue that's healthy using any common definition of the word.

BUT LET ME BE CLEAR: **THE PROBLEM ISN'T TECHNOLOGY, THE PROBLEM IS MODERATION.**

As the parents in their lives, we have to take the lead on setting technology limits for our kids, because most won't do it for themselves. Technology is like sugar in that way. Once kids get a taste, it's all they want.

I know how tough this can be. I deal with it every day—not just professionally, but with my own kid as well—and I don't always get it right.

This is still uncharted territory, and we're figuring it out at the same time they are. (And yes, it's legitimately concerning when they can't give you thirty seconds of their undivided attention, but can somehow play a video game for eight hours straight without getting up to pee).

But we can't lose sight of the fact that *we* are the ones who can effectively address this problem. In spite of their pushback, as parents we have the right and the responsibility to set healthy limits for our kids. They need us to be strong and guide them through this.

This book is the distillation of hundreds of hours of research—plus more than twenty years working with youth and families as a counselor, school administrator, and conducting parenting workshops—into simple, step-by-step, practical guidance on how to give devices a healthy, balanced place in your home.

The fact that you're reading this book already says a great deal about you as a parent. Fostering a healthy relationship between your children and technology may feel like an uphill battle at times, but if you use these tools consistently, your kids will grow into healthy young adults who have meaningful lives apart from their devices, and who can benefit from all the good that technology offers without being derailed by the bad. And that is a battle definitely worth fighting.

PART 1

DECIDE ON THE RIGHT RULES

I am going to walk you through six brief steps to decide on the right technology rules for your children. I recommend that you solidify these into a simple, clear **Family Tech Agreement**, which you can easily do using the template I've created for you at SPGbooks.com/tech

The best time to do this is undoubtedly when your children get their first devices, but if you missed this step when they were younger, don't beat yourself up—it's still doable.

I know this isn't always easy, but do your best to make sure you and your spouse are on the same page. Kids have a sixth sense for knowing when this isn't the case and capitalizing on it. It's fine to compromise or agree to disagree, but doing the upfront work to present a unified front to your children now will save you a lot of headaches later. If you're divorced, make the same effort to establish common rules and expectations. If this isn't possible, stand confidently behind *your* rules and steer clear of the differences your kids highlight between their two homes.

It's also fine to get their input as you create the agreement, but remember: *you* have the ultimate call. They need to understand that they live in a benevolent dictatorship rather than a democracy.

STEP 1:
DECIDE HOW MUCH TIME IS APPROPRIATE

One of the key components of your Family Tech Agreement will be the time limits you choose to set for your kids—but how do you decide what those limits should be? The most important consideration is how old your children are.

The recommendations below synthesize research from many sources, including the American Academy of Pediatrics, the Mayo Clinic and my own experience over two decades counseling families. Note that these guidelines do *NOT* include tech use for homework, but *DO* apply to all devices, including phones, tablets, and gaming systems.

AGE	SCHOOL DAYS	WEEKENDS, HOLIDAYS, & SUMMER
Under 18 months	No use other than video calling with relatives	
18 months to 6 years old	Up to 1 hour	Up to 1 hour
6 to 12 years old	Up to 1 hour	Up to 2 hours
12 to 15 years old	Up to 2 hours	Up to 2 hours
16 to 18 years old	Up to 2 hours	No limits—they need to learn to self-manage.

If your kids have been managing their own device use up until now, these limits may appear extreme. This may seem especially true for teenagers, since a huge part of their social life takes place through social media on their phone. This can make your job very tricky if creating hard limits leaves them feeling socially isolated at *exactly* the time they're supposed to be learning to have healthy relationships with their peers.

I stand by the numbers above as the ideal that we should strive for, but you have to make a judgement call about what is best for your child's overall social and emotional well-being. Do your best, and aim for progress over perfection. If your kids have been staying up until 2 a.m. gaming or on their phone every night, successfully shutting things down at 10 p.m. will feel like a huge victory, and that's fine. Go for the win.

Regardless of the parameters you land on, the key is to have clear limits you enforce consistently. That, more than anything, will make your effort successful.

WHEN SHOULD THEY GET THEIR OWN SMARTPHONE?

The current average age for getting a first smartphone in the United States is eleven; however, my advice is to wait until your kids are at least twelve years old (approximately the time they enter eighth grade). They may accuse you of a human rights violation, but don't worry—Amnesty International won't show up at your front door. Many parents are making the choice to wait on smartphones— including Bill Gates, by the way, who didn't allow his kids to have them until they were fourteen. If staying in contact is your concern, get them an old-school "dumb" phone that allows just talking and texting. See SPGbooks.com/tech for suggestions.

STEP 2:
DECIDE WHEN DEVICES CAN BE USED

The timeframe for device use on weekends isn't complicated, but on school days it can be. Parents who allow screen time "once homework is done" are usually frustrated by their kids rushing through their work to get their coveted screen time, which then leads to more tension. The easiest solution is to allow screen time either:

- IMMEDIATELY AFTER SCHOOL (i.e., 4 to 5 p.m.), OR
- BEFORE THEY START WINDING DOWN FOR BED (i.e., 8 to 9 p.m.)

Choosing one of these windows minimizes conflict because either they've already had their screen time when it's time to do homework, or they don't get it until 8 p.m. regardless. Some parents successfully minimize this issue even further by not allowing device use at all during the week.

Regardless of the schedule you decide on, I recommend you *do not* allow devices in their bedrooms overnight, including on weekends. A device within arm's reach is an unbearable temptation for most kids, and invariably leads to bad habits. Establish the rule that they turn in their devices at a set time each night, then charge them in a common area of the house. To minimize temptation, try to make sure desktop computers live in a common area of your home as well.

If you think they'll wait until you're asleep and then sneak more screen time, grab a laundry basket and gather up *everything* before you turn in—laptops, tablets, gaming systems, and even the screens for desktop computers—and store them in your bedroom. It may be annoying, but it's better than the alternative, and it reinforces that you make the ultimate call.

If your kids complain that they need their phones as an alarm in the morning, a basic alarm clock will run you about $10. It worked when you and I were kids, right?

WALKING OUR TALK

In our efforts to set healthy limits for our kids, we can't overlook the critical example we set. Even with the best of intentions, many parents (myself included) don't always get this right. Here's the simple truth: if we have a hard time putting our devices down, they will too. Don't believe for a second that they aren't paying attention.

Especially if they're younger, limiting devices puts more demands on us to plan activities and be engaged. Putting the kids in front of a device is almost like having free, unlimited babysitting, after all. But if we don't maintain firm limits when they're young, we'll pay the price later when bad habits are deeply entrenched.

I know this isn't always possible with work commitments, but the more you follow the same rules you give your kids, the more buy-in you will get from them. Try to wait until you kids are having their device time or are in bed before you take yours out.

STEP 3:

SET CLEAR RULES & EXPECTATIONS

Kids often confuse **rights** and **privileges**. If you think about it, their list of rights is pretty slim: love, respect, food, clothing, shelter, medical care, and a high school education. As you may have noticed, an Xbox is not on that list.

Use of technology for personal enjoyment is a privilege which should be earned by following the rules. You can establish any rules you like, of course, but below is a list of suggested nonnegotiable rules to begin with. You'll find them already preloaded into the Family Tech Agreement template for you at SPGbooks.com/tech:

1. I understand devices can only be used during the timeframes we have defined above.

2. I will not use devices during meals or special family time.

3. I understand my parents have access to all my devices, including passwords and search history, and may conduct random "safety checks."

4. I will not share my passwords with anybody other than my parents.

5. I understand my parents decide which apps can be downloaded and what video games can be played.

6. I understand all devices will be stored and charged in the place of my parents' choosing overnight. If I need an alarm clock, I'll ask them to buy me one.

7. I will not "sext" or send any other offensive or illegal images.

8. I will not use fake social media profiles or pretend to be someone else.

9. I will not search for pornography. I understand this is a weird topic to discuss with my parents, but I know I can.

10. I will not use devices or social media to bully, tease, deceive, belittle, or spread rumors about anyone.

11. I will not share my personal information (address, last name, phone number, school name, etc.) online.

12. I will work with my parents to determine the right Privacy settings for my social media accounts.

13. I will not interact with people online I don't know. If I feel harassed, bullied, or uncomfortable in any way, I will cut off all contact with that person and discuss it with my parents.

14. I will not text while driving.

STEP 4:
EQUIP YOURSELF WITH HELPFUL TOOLS

There are two key tools that will help you effectively implement your rules. I recommend starting with Option #1, and then incorporate Option #2 if that alone is not doing the job.

 ## OPTION #1:
A PARENTAL CONTROL APP

There are many options available, all of which are designed to help you be more in control of how and when your kids use their devices. For example, they can help you limit access to adult content, as well as set limits on how long your kids can use specific apps each day. See SPGbooks.com/tech for the current best options. I recommend you:

- **START WITH THE BUILT-IN TOOLS.** Smartphones already have built-in tools to assist you with this, and in many cases that will be enough. Commit to using them for one month and then decide if you need to invest in a more intensive option.

- **BE UP-FRONT ABOUT IT.** These work best when they are used out in the open, forcing honest conversations about your kids' behavior and the mutual trust in your relationship.

- RECOGNIZE THEIR LIMITATIONS. These solutions are very helpful, but still have limits. Some kids, especially as they get older, will find ways around them, so don't rely on this strategy alone. This is why you also want to gather up their devices at night, and have option #2 in your back pocket if needed.

OPTION #2:
A "DUMB" PHONE

In addition to their smartphone, you can also buy your child an inexpensive old-school "dumb" phone. If they repeatedly violate the rules and don't seem to be getting the point, they lose their smartphone and get the dumb one instead for a defined period of time (see the next step). See SPGbooks.com/tech for suggestions.

STEP 5:
DEFINE CONSEQUENCES

Make it clear to your kids what they should expect to happen if they break the rules, and also that you have the right to adjust those consequences up or down depending on the situation. Your two goals here, in this order, are:

1. Help them learn responsible online behavior.

2. Help them understand that not handling devices responsibly means they go away.

Keep it simple and try something like:

VIOLATION OF ONE OF YOUR RULES	CONSEQUENCE
1st time	• Sit-down discussion with you.
2nd time	• Loss of the device they broke the rule with for one week (i.e., loss of gaming system, taking their phone away or replacing their smartphone with the "dumb" one if they need a way to stay in touch). • Sit-down discussion with you about the choices they made.
3rd time	• Loss of the device they broke the rule with for two weeks. • Further sit-down discussion with you about the choices they made.
4th time	• Loss of the device they broke the rule with until further notice. • In order to regain use of the device, they should be able to make a clear case about what will be different moving forward. • Consider seeking the help of a professional counselor to help you get to the underlying cause of their disregard for your rules.

STEP 6:

DISCUSS YOUR FAMILY TECH AGREEMENT

Once you have decided on the right rules for your family, write them down or print out the Family Tech Agreement from the template I've provided, then make some time for a discussion with your kids. This conversation will vary depending on whether you're introducing a device into their lives for the first time, or laying down new ground rules for devices they already have.

SCENARIO 1: WHEN THEY GET THEIR FIRST DEVICES

Capitalize on the opportunity to have an honest discussion with your kids about your concerns and their questions before they begin using their first smartphone or gaming system. Say something like:

> *"Congrats! I know how excited you are to get your first phone, and I'm excited for you. I believe in you and know you're going to do your best with it, but I also want to be crystal clear about our rules and expectations. We've created this Family Tech Agreement that spells out everything you need to know. Please read it now and let's discuss."*

SCENARIO 2: THEY ALREADY HAVE DEVICES AND NEED A RESET

Use this sample script if your kids have had devices for a while and you're now resetting the rules with a Family Tech Agreement. Have the discussion a week before you implement the new agreement so they can acclimate to the idea. They still won't like it a week later, but it'll go better than saying, "Starting tonight, you'll only be able to use your phone for two hours, then it'll be in our room until tomorrow morning. By the way, how was school today, honey?" Say something like:

> *"Hey . . . we've gone back and forth about how much time you're on your phone [in front of your Xbox, etc.]. I don't want to keep fighting about it, and I'm pretty sure you don't either. Starting next week, we're going to introduce some new rules for our home. We've created a Family Tech Agreement to help us navigate this that we'd like to discuss with you. Why don't you give it a quick read and then we can go over it together."*

HANDLING OBJECTIONS

If your kids are protesting, do your best not to react emotionally or take it personally. They may say all kinds of crazy things to get you to change your mind. Don't take the bait. You're not a terrible parent. You're not the only one of their friends' parents who would do such a thing. **You're doing what is best for your family**. Keep it short and say something like:

> "I totally get that you don't like this idea and I know it will be an adjustment. It needs to happen, though, and we'll work through it together. And if your friends give you a hard time about it, you can make me the bad guy. I'm the one who is pushing this change."

If your kid is anything like mine, there's an almost constant tendency to challenge the rules. Nowhere is this more true than with setting technology limits, so we have to consistently respond in a calm but authoritative manner. This is no easy feat, but I find these two reminders helpful:

- "NO" IS A COMPLETE SENTENCE. The last thing you want is to get bogged down in an endless barrage of "Why?" questions (i.e., *Why can't I have 15 more minutes?*). If you're justifying your rules, you're losing the battle. This is where the power of "no" comes in. It's a complete sentence. It doesn't require a raised voice and it isn't punitive. Calmly say "no," then end the conversation and walk away.

- **THE 15-SECOND RULE.** When you're setting a limit or delivering a consequence, everything that needs to be said should take no more than 15 seconds. (Hence the ingenious name, "the 15-second rule.") If it takes longer than that, you're talking too much. Politely end the conversation and walk away.

Remember, endless back and forth won't get you anywhere, and contrary to your children's claims, you're not severing any of their vital limbs.

Lastly, revisit your agreement at the start of each school year to discuss what's working and what isn't. This is a perfect opportunity to reward them with more freedom and independence if they've been managing their device use well.

PART 2

TROUBLESHOOTING OBSTACLES

Your Family Tech Agreement is a great start for teaching your children responsible technology habits, but as with any parenting issue, challenges are bound to crop up. The following chapters contain practical strategies for dealing with the most common ones you're likely to face.

WHAT IF...
MY KID WON'T DO ANYTHING BUT SCREEN TIME?

If you're resetting your family's relationship to tech after bad habits have sunk in, you may be dealing with a kid who only wants to be in front of a screen. The way to address this is to push them into positive, non-digital activities. Research has shown this is an essential component of keeping kids out of trouble—whether it's hanging with the wrong crowd, experimenting with drugs and alcohol, or overdoing it with devices. Encourage (or force) them to try activities that get them out of the house, support positive social interactions, and create opportunities to engage with positive adult role models.

STEP 1: BRAINSTORM. Think through what they've done in the past or expressed an interest in, or what their friends do. Here is a list of ideas to get you started:

- Study a martial art
- Take a drawing or pottery class
- Learn an instrument
- Join a school sports team
- Join a faith based or community youth group
- Get a job or start a business cleaning out garages
- Volunteer for a political cause or not-for-profit
- Get a gym membership with a friend

STEP 2: DISCUSS WITH THEM. Say something like:

> "As we revisit how we're using devices in our family, I'd also like to see you to get involved in more activities outside the house, instead of coming home every day and plopping down in front of your Xbox for hours at a time. I'm not talking about taking it away altogether, but we can get to a better place. I've got some ideas I've been thinking about. Do you want to hear what's on my list, or think about it and then we can discuss? This has to happen, but I want to work with you to make it happen."

STEP 3: IF NECESSARY, TAKE THE LEAD. Ideally they will feel the same and make your life easy, but you may very well get the proverbial, "Nah, I'm good," as they furiously attack another Villain Lair and pop a corn chip in their mouth. If they procrastinate, these are the steps to take, from least to most intrusive:

1. *Literally* take them to stores to fill out job applications, or to a music school to sign up for guitar lessons, or to the YMCA to sign up for an after-school program.

2. Go with them to meet with their Guidance Counselor at school to see what kinds of clubs they can get involved in. This will almost certainly annoy them, but that's the cost of not taking initiative.

3. Use the "quid pro quo" approach, where you strip back their access to *all* technology until they get involved in positive things outside the house. When they do, they *earn* back screen time. For example, for every hour they're out of the house at a club, sport, or part-time job, they earn an hour of screen time. Fifteen hours per week of engagement earns fifteen hours of screen time.

STEP 4: HANDLE OBJECTIONS. If your kid is big into gaming or social media, they may try to convince you that this is their passion and that they're engaged with others, so it's the same as any other activity. The gamers may argue that this is going to be their career, and they'll be millionaires by the time they're twenty-two. Stay the course. It'll serve them much better over time. Say something like:

> *"I know this is something you love, and I'm not trying to take it away from you completely. But I want you to do more than just play video games. I know you may not like the idea, and that's OK. Some day before long you'll call your own shots, but this is something you need to go along with. I'm here to help you find other things you like too."*

WHAT IF...
DEVICES ARE TAKING OVER FAMILY TIME?

Walk into any restaurant or coffee shop these days and you'll see whole families sitting together on their phones. To get devices to a balanced place in our homes, *we* have to commit to not let this be the norm for our families. According to Common Sense Media, 41 percent of teens feel their parents get distracted by devices and don't pay attention when they're together, and 48 percent of parents admit they feel the need to immediately respond to texts, social-networking messages, and other notifications. We have to remember that our kids are always watching. If we allow ourselves to be distracted, they will follow suit.

STEP 1: MAKE MEALTIMES DEVICE-FREE. Aside from the occasional family "pizza and a movie" night, this should be a nonnegotiable. If you meet resistance, gather up all devices and keep them for a minimum of thirty minutes so there's no incentive to inhale food, avoid conversation, and get right back to business. After a few family dinners even *they'll* realize they can be off social media for thirty minutes without having a panic attack. If you're at a restaurant, leave all devices in the trunk of the car.

STEP 2: BE A STRONG ROLE MODEL. Make sure they see you doing the stuff you want them to do like reading books, being fully present when you're together, and not checking your phone every five minutes.

STEP 3: SCHEDULE INTENTIONAL, DEVICE-FREE FAMILY TIME. Few things strengthen families as much as having fun together. This can be as simple as playing a board game, throwing the ball around, or going for a hike. Needless to say, leave devices behind when you do it.

STEP 4: TROUBLESHOOT RESISTANCE. Older kids in particular may not want to hang out with you a great deal, and unfortunately there isn't much you can do to keep them from sulking and trying to make everybody else miserable. If this is happening in your family, don't let tension build around it. Instead:

1. Acknowledge that you can't force them to be all warm and fuzzy with you, but you love them and want to be connected.

2. Hold your ground about not allowing devices during meal times.

3. If they refuse to participate in family activities, be clear that there is still no device use during that time (i.e., from 2 to 4 p.m. on Sunday when the rest of you are going for a bike ride together). Lock up all devices or use your parent control app to black out their devices during that window.

STEP 5: CELEBRATE YOUR SUCCESSES. If this is a particular challenge for your family, add in some positive reinforcement by rewarding yourselves for a job well done. For instance, if you successfully make it through two weeks of device-free meals, reward yourselves with dinner out and a movie.

WHAT IF...
MY KID CAN'T MANAGE SCHOOL VS. PERSONAL USE?

Schools increasingly use online platforms to share homework assignments, textbooks and administer quizzes and tests. This has a lot of benefits, but also presents unique new challenges. A study at California State University found that 80 percent of high school students switch between studying and technology "somewhat often" to "very often." Not surprisingly, the less-distracted students had better grades. Use these strategies so you don't have to pace outside their room wondering if they're actually studying or just watching more YouTube.

STEP 1: DISCUSS. Say something like:

> *"Hey, I've noticed a number of times lately that you said you were doing your homework, but when I came in your room, you were watching YouTube. I don't want to be all up in your business, but if I see your grades falling off, I'll have to start bugging you with my own rules and restrictions. So how can I help you manage this better?"*

STEP 2: OBSERVE AND RESPOND. If they're still not managing this well themselves, here's the order of steps to take, from least to most intrusive:

1. Help them improve their "executive functioning" skills, which are tools to make them more successful at completing tasks in a timely and organized way. See SPGbooks.com/tech for more information.

2. Use your parent control app to limit what they can do online and when. For example, no access to YouTube, social media, or gaming devices until 8 p.m.

3. Ensure all homework gets done in the common areas of your home, rather than their bedroom, so you can look over their shoulder if necessary.

4. Spend time learning how their school's online platform works so you know when they actually need to be online, and when they can download and work offline.

5. You're not the only one struggling with this, so connect with other parents from your children's school to share ideas. You can also join forces and work with the school to brainstorm solutions, like sending assignments directly to *you* by email every night or providing physical textbooks.

STEP 3: DON'T MAKE YOURSELF CRAZY. If after all these steps you're still struggling to get them to take school more seriously, don't make yourself crazy. You can't force them to learn, and I've seen so many parents—with the best of intentions—severely damage their relationships battling over school. Stay the course setting healthy limits around technology, but at a certain point your children have to own their own relationship to school, and all the rewards and consequences that come with it. And remember, if they're struggling, it doesn't mean they'll wind up living in a van down by the river. *Many* kids struggle in school on their way to a bright and successful future.

WHAT IF...
MY KID IS LOOKING AT PORN?

The lure to look at pornography has tempted every generation of kids since at least the invention of the camera. According to the private research company the Barna Group, 64 percent of young people ages thirteen to twenty-four seek out porn weekly or more often. The reality is that if they're determined, you can't completely stop them from looking at it. If you shut down their access online, they'll find a way offline. Because porn is more accessible than ever, we have to be more intentional than ever in addressing it.

STEP 1: DON'T FREAK OUT. Though watching porn can lead to an unhealthy view of real relationships, the curiosity that leads kids there is completely normal. If you react too strongly, one of two things will likely happen: 1) the "taboo" you create around it will make them more curious, or 2) they'll tell you what you want to hear and get better at hiding it from you.

STEP 2: TALK ABOUT IT. Have a calm conversation. Be honest about your feelings, but do your best not to lecture. Say something like:

> *"This may be a little awkward for both of us, but I know that you were recently looking at some porn online. I'm not mad, but it is something I want to discuss with you. First, let me say that I understand your curiosity. I think all of us have it at some point. I know I did. My biggest concern, though, is that you could confuse this with what normal healthy relationships are like. But what I'd really like is to hear your thoughts."*

Then really *listen* and ask questions like:

- What do you think about what you saw?
- Do you think this is anything close to reality?
- Do you think this could be harmful to any of the people involved? Or any of the people watching it?
- Do you think this helps or hurts your chances of having a healthy relationship with someone you care about?

STEP 3: EDUCATE. Watch a few videos about the harmful effects of pornography with them (see the SPGbooks. com/tech for suggestions).

STEP 4: MONITOR. Use your parent control app for all your household devices. Be clear that while you can't completely prevent them from watching it, you're going to do your best to keep pornography away from your family.

STEP 5: GET THEM HELP. If it's a recurring issue and you think your kids are at risk for addiction, get them help. See SPGbooks.com/tech for suggestions.

WHAT IF...
MY KID IS BEING BULLIED ONLINE?

Bullying has always been a difficult thing kids deal with, and in the digital age it's more challenging than ever. According to cyberbullying.org, approximately 37 percent of young people between the ages of twelve and seventeen have been bullied online. Understandably, many parents' greatest fear is that their child will be on the receiving end of this painful behavior, and will feel isolated and unsure who they can turn to. There may be no way to completely prevent bullying, but there are clear things we can do to minimize its damaging effect.

STEP 1: LISTEN AND SUPPORT. The most important thing to do is listen without judgement. Your child may be unsure about sharing what's happening with you in the first place, either out of embarrassment or out of fear that getting you involved will somehow make things worse. Make sure they know you're grateful they told you, that you're in their corner no matter what, and that you'll work *with* them to end it. Don't punish them if they were on a site or app they shouldn't have been on, but do revisit it later as a "teaching moment" when the dust has settled.

STEP 2: HELP THEM PROTECT THEMSELVES. More than anything, they need to understand that the bully's behavior isn't about them; it's about the bully. People bully because they're inwardly insecure, and don't know a better way to feel good about themselves. Therefore the best thing to do is not retaliate; instead, ignore them and block all further communication. Bullies require a victim. If your child is unavailable to play that role, the bullying will stop.

STEP 3: ESCALATE IF NECESSARY. If the bullying continues, or transfers from online to in person, here are the steps to take, from least to most intensive. Reassure your child that you'll move at their pace. They need to feel some control over the process to ease their fear that it'll get worse. Also make sure to take screenshots so you have clear evidence about what's taking place.

1. If you know the bully's parents, and you're confident you can have a productive conversation with them, reach out and get their help in ending the behavior.

2. Contact your child's guidance counselor at school, or whoever is in charge of disciplinary measures. Most schools today have bullying policies that extend to online behavior, and they will be supportive in addressing the issue.

3. Laws vary from state to state, but the cyberbullying may very well be illegal, so if it persists, contact the police. They will help you understand the law and what support they can offer.

STEP 4: HELP THEM BUILD THEIR SELF-CONFIDENCE. If your child's confidence has taken a blow as a result of the bullying, help them engage in offline activities that will boost it. See *"What If . . .My Kids Don't Want to do Anything But Screen Time?"* The same basic principle applies here. Also encourage them to take a break from social media. Some time away will give them perspective, and will help them see the bully's behavior for what it is—an unkind act from somebody desperately trying to feel good about themselves. For additional resources, see SPGbooks. com/tech.

WHAT IF...
MY KID IS THE BULLY?

Finding out your child is doing the bullying is just as painful as learning they're on the receiving end of it. It's the opposite of what any parent wants to hear and believe about their child, and it's very difficult not to feel that it reflects poorly on you as a parent. That said, all kids are capable of bullying, and it doesn't mean they're bad people with bleak futures. If you take it seriously and address it head on *now*, the behavior can be corrected.

STEP 1: STAY CALM AND GET MORE INFO. Before confronting your child, get as much information as possible. Did it happen once with one child, or with multiple kids over time? Was it only online, or in person as well? Which apps were used? Were pictures sent? Get hard evidence if you can (for example, screenshots of social media posts).

STEP 2: REFLECT ON WHY IT MAY BE HAPPENING. There is no good excuse for this behavior, but bullies need empathy as much as their victims so we can help them stop bullying. Kids typically behave this way for one of two reasons:

1. They're getting positive feedback from others (such as making them laugh), which temporarily helps them feel good about themselves.

2. They're hurting inside, and acting this way makes them feel more powerful and in control. They might be getting bullied themselves, suffering from low self-esteem, or dealing with a specific, painful situation, like divorce or a death in the family.

STEP 3: DISCUSS. Calmly lay out the facts you've gathered. Be clear that this behavior is not acceptable, but that you're also concerned about *them*, and why they chose to do this. Say something like:

> *"I love you and I'm in your corner no matter what, but this behavior is not OK. I know you're better than this, and this is not consistent with our values as a family. Now please help me understand what's going on that caused you to behave this way."*

STEP 4: HOLD THEM ACCOUNTABLE TO RIGHT THEIR WRONG. In addition to following the consequences laid out in your Family Tech Agreement, help them make amends with the target of their bullying. Their actions should be meaningful and should make them uncomfortable. For example, you can require them to apologize in person, or to go with you to school to discuss it with an administrator, and maybe the target and their parents as well, if appropriate.

STEP 5: BE SUPPORTIVE AND VIGILANT. Based on what you discovered in Step 2, help them find positive ways to feel good about themselves. Explore extracurricular activities where they can work on healthy friendship skills and find positive leadership opportunities. If the problem continues, seek professional help. The negative long-term effects of being a bully are too severe to not do everything you can to help them. For additional resources, see SPGbooks.com/tech.

WHAT IF...
MY KID IS BEING UNSAFE ONLINE?

Just as they do offline, kids are going to make mistakes online. As much as we try to prevent it, they'll say or post something they shouldn't, and in some cases engage with people they should be avoiding. Hopefully they won't go too far, but pushing the limits is what kids are wired to do. What matters more than *them* making a mistake is how *we* handle it. By using these tools, we'll support them as best we can on their journey to become mature "digital citizens."

STEP 1: FOLLOW YOUR FAMILY TECH AGREEMENT. You've already done the hard work of thinking this through, putting it in writing, and communicating with them about it. Now is the time to rely on it and follow your plan.

STEP 2: FOCUS ON YOUR RELATIONSHIP. It's impossible to have control over your children when they're sitting right next to you, let alone when they're off on their own. However, if you put in the time to keep your relationship strong, you'll wind up with something just as valuable: *influence*. They still won't tell you everything (we're talking about kids, after all), but when the big things hit—and they always hit—you'll be one of the people they talk to. If they get into deeper water than they can handle online, a strong relationship with you is the single greatest asset they'll have working in their favor.

STEP 3: TAKE ACTION IF STRANGERS CONTACT THEM.
According to the University of New Hampshire's Youth Internet Safety Study, 9 percent of kids who use the internet receive an unwanted sexual solicitation, and 4 percent of predators try to make offline contact. Teens who are hungry for attention are susceptible to letting their guard down once they feel they can trust someone, so we need to be alert. The most frequent targets are girls ages twelve to fifteen, teen boys who are questioning their sexuality, and kids who are socially isolated. Have a conversation where you say something like:

"Hey, I want to talk to you about staying safe online. It's possible a complete stranger will contact you and try to make you think they're someone who really cares. They may even want to meet you face-to-face. If this ever happens, no matter how much you think you can trust them, please talk to me about it right away, especially if that person tries to talk about sex or asks for pictures of you. If you're 100 percent convinced this is a legit person who's your age and who you want to meet in person, then let me come with you. Do you have any questions about this?"

If you've confirmed they've had inappropriate communication with an adult online, help them sever all communication with that person immediately and contact your local police department. You'll be protecting your child and any others that person is targeting. For more resources, see SPGbooks.com/tech.

STEP 4: HELP THEM LEARN FROM THEIR MISTAKES.
The writer Samuel Smiles said, *"We learn wisdom from failure much more than from success."* If our children make mistakes, we of course have to hold them accountable, but we also have to supportively be in their corner as they work through it. By gently asking questions like, *"So what can you learn from this?"* we'll help them start to gain that much-needed wisdom.

STEP 5: GET PROFESSIONAL HELP. If the problem persists, it suggests there is a deeper issue going on that they need help resolving. Seek out the services of a professional counselor.

WHAT IF...

I'VE LOST CONTROL OF MY KID'S DEVICE USE?

In an ideal world I wouldn't have to address this, but I've talked to enough parents whose kids have kicked a hole in the wall or threatened to harm themselves when they tried to set limits that it's necessary. If this is the case in your household, I understand how scary it is, but it needs to be addressed head-on.

IF THEY THREATEN YOU OR YOUR PROPERTY

If they threaten you or your property, involve the police. I get it: *nobody* wants to call the police on their child, but if they're trying to control your home through threat and intimidation, it's the smartest thing you can do—for everybody. It will bring sanity back to your home, and will teach them the critical life lesson that they can't go around threatening others. **Take these steps:**

1. CONTACT YOUR LOCAL JUVENILE OFFICER. Go in person or call the non-emergency number of your local police department and ask for the juvenile officer. Explain your situation, ask how they've dealt with similar situations, and find out what support they can offer. Get their contact information and stay in touch.

2. DISCUSS WITH YOUR CHILD. Reassure them that you love them and are committed to working together to get things to a better place, but be clear

that moving forward any kind of physical force used against your family or property will not be tolerated. The police will be called.

3. CALL 911. If they don't heed your warning and become violent, call 911. Just the appearance of a police officer will de-escalate the situation and show you mean business. It's quite possible the officer who shows up won't be the same one you spoke to, so share that you've spoken with the juvenile officer and they know about your situation. They will usually take that as a cue to respond in a supportive way.

4. FOLLOW UP. Stay in touch with the juvenile officer and let them know what happened. Build this relationship and follow up as needed. Calling 911 isn't something you should have to do on a regular basis, but be willing to go there in the face of physical aggression to reclaim your home.

IF THEY THREATEN TO HARM THEMSELVES

If a child threatens to harm themselves over device limits, one of two things is true: 1) They're really in a crisis and need help, or 2) They're trying to manipulate you, in which case they need to learn this is not OK. Either way, take it seriously. **Be loving but firm, and take these steps:**

1. ADDRESS IT HEAD-ON. Say: "*Look, if you're serious about that, we're going to the hospital now to have you evaluated and maybe committed. I love you and I'm not going to risk losing you. If I hear that from you again, be ready to pack your bags.*"

2. FOLLOW THROUGH. Have a zero-tolerance policy for these kind of threats. More likely than not your child is trying to manipulate you, but it's not something you want to play around with.

FINAL THOUGHTS

If you use the tools in this book consistently, you *will* help your family find a healthy technology balance. It won't always be easy but you can do this, and the payoff will be worth it. You'll significantly reduce the day-to-day tension in your home, and you'll have more positive family time that isn't dominated by devices. Most of all, you'll give your kids the gift of knowing how to manage their technology in a healthy and responsible way. That's an invaluable skill that will last them a lifetime.

LOOKING FOR MORE SIMPLE PARENTING RESOURCES?

To get our free mini-course: *How to Help Your Child Thrive* please visit **SPGbooks.com/course**

ABOUT THE AUTHOR

Joshua Wayne has been working with youth and families for over 20 years in schools, mental health agencies, the foster care system, as well as in private practice. He speaks to students around the world about tech, mental health and good decision-making, and to the adults in their lives about how to help them thrive as they transition to adulthood. To invite him to speak at your next event, visit joshuawayne.com/speaking.

Made in the USA
San Bernardino, CA
02 June 2020

72614745R00024